Happy Cooking!

Debbie Cornwell

published by
Wellton Books

P.O. Box 989
Citrus Heights CA 95611

SBN   0-943678-005

Printed in U.S.A.—1

artprint press
Sacramento, California

COOKING IN THE NUDE
for playful gourmets

Written and illustrated by
Debbie & Stephen Cornwell

CAUTION . . . . .

Cooking in the Nude is intended for lovers and potential lovers. Excessive use of this book may result in loss of sleep. We suggest you reserve these recipes for only the most special occasions.

REMEMBER . . . . .

Attitude and ambiance are primary ingredients to seductive dining. Before trying the first recipe, you should read the sections on setting the mood and presentation. Then, stylize our ideas to fit your own personality, as well as the occasion.

TO ENJOY . . . . .

each experience to its fullest, approach every recipe as the beginning of a new and uniquely exciting evening of seduction. Menu recommendations are provided with each entree. You'll note that we seldom make mention of desserts — how you conclude each evening of dining is left totally to your imagination!

COOKING IN THE NUDE . . . . .

is a fun book which offers a variety of recipes to please any palate. Special attention is given to appearance and presentation of each entree. The book is the perfect collection of sensual dining experiences for two. The format is both fun and lusty — we encourage both!

CONTENTS

CHEAP FRILLS

(Creating the Mood)

Creating an atmosphere of intimacy and intrigue will captivate your intended lover even before the first course is served. The tactics which you employ will depend on your personality and intentions. Is your guest a new acquaintance, your spouse, or something in between? If your companion is familiar with your environment and style of dining, creating the mood may involve a change in both. If the relationship is already intimate, what would you do differently if this were the evening of first seduction? Get the picture? Sure you do! Lusty thoughts, everything special, setting the mood to realize your fantasy.

And it doesn't take that much effort to tablecloth the table, accent your setting with fresh flowers, and to lower the lighting. A dimmer switch is a great cheap frill!

Your next step should be an excursion in self-expression. Table linens reflect your moods and can provide a very subtle, yet unmistakable, suggestion to your companion. Start with a solid color tablecloth. For versatility, buy several sets of napkins. Choose your patterns to express your variable and capricious nature. For example:
— an amorous and sultry tropical print in deliciously deep rich colors (purple, violet, fuchsia, crimson) conveying an aura of clandestine intrigue
— a sporty adventurous print in bright, vivid, spirited colors and patterns that are bold and confident
— a tantalizing and passionate print, pulsating with vibrant unleashed color and designs which reveal your creativity and curiosity.

To complete the mise-en-scene, add fresh flowers, candlelight, or arrange fresh fruit on a board or in a basket. Don't forget the obvious — taking the phone off the hook, getting rid of the kids (if any) for the evening, and the selection of music; television is very counter-productive to seduction.

DOES SIZE REALLY MATTER?

(PRESENTATION)

It has probably been debated since Adam first cooked for Eve, however, it most definitely matters when it comes to an appropriate selection of serving pieces and stemware. Au gratin dishes are recommended for many of our recipes ... the 9″ size is superb for entrees, while the 5″ is perfect for something on the side. An assortment of either ramekins, pedestal dessert dishes or small bowls is also a must for proper presentation of individual sauces, dressings, and condiments. Now we're not suggesting you throw away your everyday dishes or pull the china out of the closet — just add some variety to what you usually use and keep the mayonnaise jar off the table. Play the best shot your pocketbook can afford and remember your objective!

BEFORE PLAY

(Pantry Needs)

Your pantry must become the catalyst for adventurous dining endeavors. Each recipe which follows will include its own suggestions for seasonings and garnishes. Tailor them to your own tastes and experiment. Do not be afraid to take culinary license. Explore all possibilities and give in to whimsey! (Nothing ventured, nothing gained!) A well-stocked pantry, including the following list of seasonings and garnishes, will allow you the versatility to prepare all of our recipes.

<table>
<tr><td>croutons</td><td>olive oil</td></tr>
<tr><td>walnuts</td><td>Dijon mustard</td></tr>
<tr><td>pecans</td><td>ginger</td></tr>
<tr><td>slivered almonds</td><td>curry</td></tr>
<tr><td>sunflower seeds</td><td>tarragon</td></tr>
<tr><td>raisins</td><td>fennel seed</td></tr>
<tr><td>chutney</td><td>cayenne</td></tr>
<tr><td>black olives</td><td>dill</td></tr>
<tr><td>artichoke hearts</td><td>nutmeg</td></tr>
<tr><td>artichoke crowns</td><td>beau monde</td></tr>
<tr><td>marinated mushrooms</td><td>grated orange peel</td></tr>
<tr><td>fresh mushrooms</td><td>grated lemon peel</td></tr>
<tr><td>fresh parsley</td><td>sherry</td></tr>
<tr><td>lemons</td><td>port</td></tr>
<tr><td>canned fruits</td><td>marsala</td></tr>
<tr><td></td><td>brandy</td></tr>
<tr><td></td><td>burgundy</td></tr>
<tr><td></td><td>white wine (sauterne,
  if available)</td></tr>
<tr><td></td><td>vermouth</td></tr>
</table>

APPETEASERS

ESCARGOT IN CAPS

STEP ONE: 10 min.

1/2 C. butter (1 stick)
2 T. parsley, chopped
2 cloves garlic, minced
1 t. onion, minced
salt and pepper
dash of nutmeg

Melt butter. Add remaining ingredients. Mix well.

STEP TWO: 15 min.

1 can escargot, rinsed and drained
24 medium mushrooms, stems removed
juice of 1/2 lemon

Squeeze lemon juice over mushroom caps. Place a dab of seasoned butter in each cap. Place 1 escargot in each cap. Cover each escargot with remaining seasoned butter and place on baking sheet or escargot plates. Heat in oven until butter bubbles.

WALNUT STUFFED MUSHROOMS

STEP ONE: 15 min.

18 medium mushrooms
4 T. butter
1/2 C. walnuts, chopped
1/4 C. onions, minced
1 clove garlic, minced

Remove stems from mushrooms. Reserve and chop 1 cup of stems, set aside. In large fry pan, melt butter and saute walnuts for 4 minutes. Remove walnuts, add mushroom stems, onions, and garlic. Saute 5-8 min.

STEP TWO: 20 min.

1/4 C. fresh bread crumbs
1 T. parsley, chopped
1/4 t. pepper
2 pinches cayenne

In bowl, combine all ingredients, except caps, and mix well. Place caps on broiler pan and stuff with filling. Bake at 350° for 15 min.

These may be served as appeteasers or in place of a traditional vegetable side dish.

HOT 'N SWEET

STEP ONE: 15 min.

1 can pineapple chunks, in heavy syrup
1/2 C. brown sugar
1/4 C. lemon juice
2 T. cornstarch
1 t. prepared mustard

Drain and reserve syrup from pineapple. Combine syrup and all remaining ingredients, except pineapple chunks, in small saucepan. Stir over medium heat until thickened.

STEP TWO: 2 min.

2 C. cubed ham
pineapple chunks

Add ham and pineapple to pan. Stir until hot. Serve on toothpicks.

CREAM CHEESE BALLS

STEP ONE: 40 min.

1 8 oz. pkg. cream cheese
1 T. mayonnaise
1/2 t. worcestershire
1 T. dry minced onion
1/4 C. black olives, chopped

Soften cream cheese. Add remaining ingredients. Chill in refrigerator for 20-30 min., then remove and roll into a ball.

STEP TWO: 2 min.

3/4 C. walnuts, chopped
4 sprigs of parsley

Roll cheese ball in nuts and wrap in plastic wrap. Chill until ready to use. To serve, place ball in center of plate, tuck parsley sprigs under edges of ball and ring plate with crackers.

CHUTNEY & HAM STUFFED MUSHROOMS

STEP ONE: 1 hr. 20 min.

10 large mushrooms
1/2 lemon
1/2 C. chopped ham
1 T. Dijon mustard
1 T. chutney, minced
1 T. sour cream, rounded
1 T. mayonnaise, rounded
1 t. vinegar
1 t. dry onion, minced
4 sprigs of parsley

Remove stems from mushrooms and sprinkle caps with lemon juice. Combine remaining ingredients, except parsley, and fill caps. Chill 1 hour. To serve, place caps on plate and tuck parsley around caps.

These can be served as an appeteaser or in place of a dinner salad.

LETTUCE BE LOVERS

Your salad can be as provocative as your entree, whether served as the introduction or the conclusion of your meal. It should delight the eye of your epicurean companion, suggesting the uniqueness of the hours that lie ahead. This can be a simple accomplishment on your part, yet, dazzle your intended lover with your attention to detail. The subtle nuances are best expressed by an uninhibited spirit. We offer the following suggestions only as a guide to basic composition — Be original and let your creative juices flow!

STEP ONE: 3 min.

1 part fresh spinach
2 parts red leaf lettuce

Wash and tear greens and put them into a large salad bowl.

STEP TWO: 4 min.

3 T. butter
1/2 C. croutons
3 T. parmesan

Melt butter, add croutons and toss until coated. Put parmesan in plastic bag. Add croutons and shake. Add croutons to greens and toss well.

STEP THREE: 5-10 min.

any combination of three garnishes (see Before Play)
salad dressing

Arrange 3 garnishes on a salad plate and top with serving spoon or tongs. Chill. Serve dressing in individual bowls or cruet. You and your guest may now create your salads individually, with fun and flair.

APPETEASER
walnut stuffed mushrooms

SALAD
with shrimp garnish

PIECE DE NO RESISTANCE
flirtatious fillets

ON THE SIDE
broccoli in lemon sauce

chenin blanc

PIECE DE NO RESISTANCE

FLIRTATIOUS FILLETS

Flirting can pay, and go a long way . . . just be prepared to roll in the hay.

STEP ONE: 7 min.

2 T. butter	Melt butter in large fry pan and saute
3/4 C. mushrooms, sliced	mushrooms and onion for 5 min.
1 small onion, chopped	

STEP TWO: 40 min.

1/2 lb. fillet of sole (dry well with paper towels)	Lightly grease two au gratin dishes. Arrange fillets in dishes. Pour vermouth
1/4 C. vermouth	over fish and dot with butter. Season
2 T. butter	with salt, pepper, and tarragon. Spoon
1 t. tarragon	mushroom melange over fish, cover
salt and pepper	with foil and bake at 350° for 35 min.

PEEL ME A GRAPE

We couldn't remember if this was what Cleopatra said to Marc Anthony or if Mae West coined the phrase. We are sure that whoever said it knew what they were suggesting!

STEP ONE: 3 min.

1/2 lb. fillet of sole (dry well with paper towels)

Place fillets in greased au gratin dishes.

STEP TWO: 10 min.

1 T. butter
3 large mushrooms, sliced
1 C. white grapes
1/4 C. sour cream
1/4 C. mayonnaise
1 t. lemon juice

Melt butter in small pan over low heat. Saute mushrooms 3-5 min. Add grapes, heat through, stir gently. Add remaining ingredients, stirring until blended.

STEP THREE: 20 min.

Spoon sauce over fillets. Cover au gratins with foil and bake at 325° for 20 min.

ham and chutney mushrooms

waldorf salad

peel me a grape

broccoli in lemon sauce

chenin blanc

cream cheese ball

salad with shrimp
and chilled asparagus

wild rice

fantasies au fruits
de mer

pinot blanc

FANTASIES AU FRUITS DE MER

Ancient mariners have long had fantasies of the deep. To what depths do your fantasies go?

STEP ONE: 10 min.

1 lb. scallops, cut to bite-size	Shake scallops and flour in a plastic bag until scallops are evenly coated. Melt butter in fry pan and lightly brown scallops over medium heat.
1/4 C. flour	
1/4 C. butter	

STEP TWO: 15 min.

1/2 C. butter	Melt butter in a clean pan. Saute onion for 5 min. Add mushrooms and garlic. Season with salt and pepper. Continue to saute for 4 min. Add scallops, lemon juice, and wine. Simmer 4 min. or until heated through.
1 small white onion, minced	
1 1/2 lb. mushrooms, sliced	
1 T. garlic, minced	
1 t. salt	
1/2 t. white pepper	
1 T. lemon juice	
1 C. white wine	

A LITTLE DILL WILL DO . . .

and so, probably, will your lover. This quickie to fix will assure you plenty of time after dinner to find out.

STEP ONE: 5 min.

1 lg. salmon steak
pinch of dill
salt and pepper

Cut salmon in half and lay half in each of two au gratin dishes. Season with dill, salt, and pepper.

STEP TWO: 20 min.

1 can new potatoes
1 small jar of artichoke hearts

Arrange 2-3 potatoes on one side of fish. Drain artichoke marinade over fish and potatoes, and reserve hearts. Bake at 400° for 10-12 min.

STEP THREE: 4 min.

artichoke hearts
2 sprigs fresh dill (or parsley)
2 lemon slices (split from edge of peel to center and twist)

Garnish fish and potatoes with hearts and dill. Place a lemon twist on top of fish.

cream cheeseball

scalloped mushrooms
and almonds

honey glazed
acorn squash

a little dill will do

pinot blanc

escargot in caps

hot spinach salad

carnal coq au vin

broccoli in lemon sauce

wild rice

fume blanc

CARNAL COQ AU VIN

Treat your lustier appetite to this classic feast and see what happens!

STEP ONE: 3 min.

1/2 C. flour
1/2 t. salt
1/4 t. pepper
1/2 t. beau monde
1 cut up fryer

Fill a plastic bag with flour and seasonings. Add chicken and shake to coat.

STEP TWO: 15 min.

1/2 C. oil
1 clove garlic, minced

Add oil to fry pan and saute garlic over low heat for 2 minutes. Add chicken and brown it on all sides. Remove chicken to a glass baking dish and arrange in a single layer.

STEP THREE: 1 hr.

1 C. mushrooms, sliced
2 T. parsley, chopped
1 C. white wine

Saute mushrooms in remaining oil for 5 minutes. Add parsley and wine. Pour this mixture over chicken and bake at 350° for 45 min. - 1 hr.

STEP FOUR: 3 min.

2 sprigs of fresh parsley

Remove chicken pieces to au gratin dishes and garnish with parsley.

CHICKEN APHRODESIA

Gives the rooster a booster and the chicken, a delight.

STEP ONE: 20 min.

1 cut up fryer, over 3 lb.
1/4 C. butter
1 C. mushrooms, sliced

Brown chicken in butter over medium heat. Remove to a casserole. Add mushrooms to pan and saute 3-5 minutes. Scatter mushrooms over chicken.

STEP TWO: 50 min.

2 T. flour
1 1/4 C. orange juice
2 T. brown sugar
1 t. salt
1/2 t. ginger
1 t. dry mustard

Turn heat to low and whisk in flour (you may need to alternate flour and orange juice to avoid lumps). Add remaining ingredients and turn heat to medium, stirring constantly until thickened. Pour over chicken and bake at 350° for 45 min., baste.

STEP THREE: 3 min.

1 small can manderin oranges
2 T. parsley, chopped

Remove chicken and mushrooms to two au gratins, arrange orange sections on top, and sprinkle with parsley.

chutney and ham
stuffed mushrooms

salad with
chilled asparagus

chicken aphrodesia

honey glazed
acorn squash

chenin blanc

APPETEASER
  hot and sweet

LETTUCE BE LOVERS
  caesar salad

PIECE DE NO RESISTANCE
  exotic erotic chicken
  in bed with wild rice

ON THE SIDE
  ginger glazed carrots

  riesling

EXOTIC EROTIC CHICKEN

Set the trap with exotic bait . . . and erotic game may be your catch.

STEP ONE: 10 min.

2 whole chicken breasts

Skin , bone, and split breasts, then flatten with mallet.

STEP TWO: 5 min.

6 T. butter
2 T. Dijon mustard
1 1/2 C. walnuts, finely chopped

Melt butter in small saucepan. Stir in mustard. Dip each piece of chicken in mustard, then pat walnuts on each piece, coating heavily.

STEP THREE: 8 min.

4 T. butter
2 T. oil

Melt butter and oil in large fry pan. Add chicken pieces and saute 3-5 min. per side. Remove chicken to platter.

STEP FOUR: 2 min.

1/2 C. sour cream
1 T. Dijon mustard
dash of pepper

Spoon leftover walnuts onto chicken and pour off oil in pan. Add sour cream and mustard to pan stirring until smooth and hot. Stir in pepper.

STEP FIVE: 1 min.

parsley sprigs

Place chicken pieces in warmed au gratins. Spoon a small amount of sauce over chicken and garnish with parsley.

27

BREAST OF CALYPSO

Greek legend has it that a sea nymph, Calypso, promised her lovers immortality if they would never leave her. You, of course, should negotiate your own terms!

STEP ONE: 1 hr. 10 min.

3 T. olive oil
1 T. butter
1 sm. onion, minced
1 can stewed tomatoes
1/4 C. tomato juice
1/4 C Marsala
1/4 t. coriander
1/4 t. fennel seed
1/4 t. bay leaf, crumpled
1/2 t. basil
1/2 t. oregano
1/2 t. thyme
pinch orange peel
parsley, minced

Heat oil and butter in large fry pan over medium heat, add onion and saute 5 min. Stir in remaining ingredients except parsley, and simmer 1 hr. Remove pan from heat, stir in parsley, and set aside. 15 min. prior to end of cooking time, start Step Two.

STEP TWO: 20 min.

3 T. butter
2-3 chicken breasts
5-6 T. parmesan

Heat butter in a 10" fry pan. Add chicken breasts and saute 5-8 min. per side (or until done). Transfer breasts to au gratin dishes, spoon sauce over breasts and sprinkle with parmesan. Put under broiler until cheese bubbles, then serve.

fresh spinach salad

walnut stuffed mushrooms

honey glazed acorn squash

breast of calypso

pinot blanc

salad du jour

honey glazed
acorn squash

broccoli in
lemon sauce

birds in bondage

sauvignon blanc

BIRDS IN BONDAGE

Decidely kinky! Reserve this one for only your most uninhibited evenings!

STEP ONE: 20 min.

4-8 boned chicken thighs (or breasts)
2 C. cooked wild rice (or bread crumbs)
1/4 C. raisins
1/2 C. walnuts, chopped

Flatten chicken pieces with mallet or rolling pin. Place equal amounts of rice, raisins, and nuts on each piece and roll up, jelly-roll fashion. Secure with thread or toothpicks.

STEP TWO: 30 min.

2 T. butter
1/4 C. water

Heat butter in large fry pan and brown chicken rolls over medium heat. Add water, cover and simmer 15 min.

STEP THREE: 20 min.

1/4 C. packed brown sugar
2 T. cornstarch
1/4 t. cinnamon
1 3/4 C. water
1 t. lemon juice
1 t. salt
1/2 C. raisins

Remove chicken rolls to a plate. Mix sugar, cornstarch and cinnamon together, and stir into liquid in pan. Add remaining ingredients and bring to a boil, stirring until thickened. Remove thread or toothpicks from chicken and return to pan. Cover and heat thoroughly.

STEP FOUR: 2 min.

2 T. parsley
2 C. cooked wild rice

Arrange a bed of wild rice in 2 au gratin dishes. Place rolls on a bed of rice, spoon sauce over rolls and garnish with parsley.

ADAM'S SWEET DEMISE

could lead to your own, if you're willing to share a rib with a guest.

STEP ONE: 15 min.

1 lb. boneless beef short ribs
2 T. shortening
1/2 t. salt
1/4 t. pepper
1 medium onion, quartered

Brown ribs in shortening and pour off drippings. Season with salt and pepper. Add onion.

STEP TWO: 2 hr.

1/2 C. brown sugar
1 t. dry mustard
1/2 C. raisins
1 T. flour
2 T. vinegar
1/4 t. grated lemon peel
1 bay leaf
1 1/2 C. water

Combine all ingredients in a small saucepan and bring to a boil. Pour over ribs, cover, and simmer on low heat for 2 hours. Remove ribs to a serving dish or au gratins and place in low oven to keep warm.

STEP THREE: 5 min.

2 T. flour
1/4-1/2 C. hot water
2 sprigs parsley

Mix flour and water in a jar. Whisk it into sauce. Turn heat to medium and stir until thickened. Pour sauce over ribs and garnish with parsley.

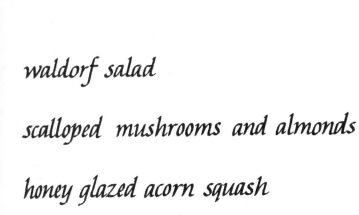

waldorf salad

scalloped mushrooms and almonds

honey glazed acorn squash

adams sweet demise

gamay beaujolais

walnut stuffed mushrooms

salad greens with cauliflower
and artichoke heart garnish

simmering denouement

scalloped mushrooms
and almonds

cabernet sauvignon

SIMMERING DENOUEMENT

A classic French meal which may inspire the sensual appetite, simmering slowly to a fulfilling denouement.

STEP ONE: 15 min.

1/4 C. flour
1 lb. lean stew meat, cut to bite-size
1 onion, minced
1 clove garlic, minced
3 T. oil

Add flour and beef to a plastic bag and shake. In large fry pan, saute onion and garlic in oil for 5 minutes. Add beef and brown over medium heat.

STEP TWO: 1 hr.

2 C. water
2 beef bouillion cubes
1/2 t. salt
1/2 t. thyme
1/4 t. pepper
1 t. oregano
1 t. basil
1 bay leaf

Stir all ingredients into fry pan, loosen bits from bottom of pan, cover and simmer over low heat 1 hr.

STEP THREE: 35 min.

1 C. carrots, sliced
1 C. mushroom caps
1/4 C. parsley
1/2 C. burgundy
2 C. cooked noodles

Add carrots and mushrooms, and continue to cook 30 min. At end of cooking time, stir in parsley and wine. Heat through for 5 min. Serve in au gratin dishes over buttered and parsleyed noodles.

AFFAIRE NOUVEAU

We do not what we ought, what we ought not, we do, and lean upon the thought that chance will bring us through! Good Luck!

STEP ONE: 10 min.

1/3 C. diced salt pork, rind removed and reserved
1 large onion, chopped
3 shallots, chopped

Cook salt pork in heavy skillet over medium heat, until golden. Remove with slotted spoon to small dutch oven. Add onion and shallot to fry pan and brown over high heat. Remove to dutch oven with slotted spoon.

STEP TWO: 20 min.

1/2 C. flour
1-2 lb. lean stew meat, cut in bite-size cubes
1-2 T. butter

Shake flour and beef in plastic bag until coated evenly. Add beef to fry pan and brown well on all sides (do not let cubes touch or they will steam instead of brown).
Transfer beef to dutch oven.

STEP THREE: 2-3 hrs.

1/4 C. Cognac
2 C. beef stock
1 T. Dijon mustard
pork rind

Pour Cognac in fry pan and cook over medium heat until a glaze of liquid is all that remains. Stir in beef stock and boil. Stir in Dijon and pour into dutch oven. Add rind. Bring to a simmer, cover loosly and cook 2-3 hrs.

STEP FOUR: 10 min.

2 large carrots cut to bite-size
2 T. butter
1 C. small mushrooms
1/4 C. burgundy

Add carrots 30 min. prior to end of cooking time. Bring stew to simmer. Heat butter in fry pan, add mushrooms and brown well. Add wine and boil 20 sec. Stir stew and simmer 5 min.

escargot in caps

spinach salad vinaigrette

affaire nouveau

scalloped mushrooms
   and almonds

gamay beaujolais

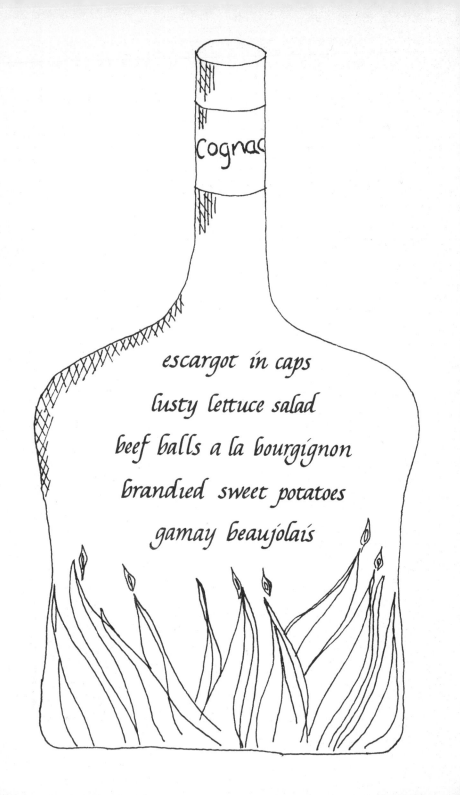

Cognac

escargot in caps

lusty lettuce salad

beef balls a la bourgignon

brandied sweet potatoes

gamay beaujolais

BEEF BALLS A LA BOURGIGNON

When you're feeling less than subtle, try putting this one on the table.

STEP ONE: 20 min.

1 lb. lean ground beef	Throroughly mix meat and seasonings. Shape into 1" balls and brown evenly in butter.
1 t. salt	
1/4 t. pepper	
1 t. fines herbes	
1/2 t. marjoram	
1/4 t. rosemary	
1 T. butter	

STEP TWO: 4 min.

3 T. brandy	Heat brandy in small pan, pour over beef and ignite. When flame dies, remove beef to bowl.

STEP THREE: 10 min.

1/2 lb. small whole mushrooms	Add mushrooms to pan and saute 5 minutes, then remove to bowl. Repeat process with onions and remove.
1/2 lb. small white onions, peeled	

STEP FOUR: 30 min.

2 T. flour	Stir flour into drippings with whisk. Add liquids slowly, blend well. Add remaining ingredients, stir until thickened. Simmer 8 minutes. Add beef, onions, and mushrooms. Cover and simmer 20 minutes, stirring occasionally. Serve in au gratin dishes over buttered noodles tossed with parsley.
1/2 C. canned beef broth	
1 C. burgundy	
1/2 C. port	
2 T. tomato paste	
1 bay leaf	

VOYEURS VENTUROUS VEAL BIRDS

will excite the palate and the eye, but be careful . . . your epicurean friend may want to leave the lights on after dinner.

STEP ONE: 20 min.

2 strips bacon, fried and crumpled
1 T. parsley, minced
1 clove garlic, minced
1 C. cooked wild rice (or fresh bread crumbs)
1 egg
1 lb. veal fillets*, thinly sliced

Mix bacon, parsley, garlic, rice, and egg together. Spoon mixture onto veal slices and roll up tightly. Secure with thread or toothpicks.

STEP TWO: 1 hr. 10 min.

2 T. butter
1 T. flour
2/3 C. chicken broth
2/3 C. white wine
salt and pepper to taste

Melt butter in a large fry pan. Add veal birds and brown quickly over medium heat. Remove birds to a dish. Add flour to pan and whisk until smooth. Blend in remaining ingredients and bring to a boil. Return birds to pan, cover and simmer on low heat 1 hour.

STEP THREE: 0

1 1/2 C. sliced mushrooms
1 firm tomato, quartered (optional)
sprigs of fresh parsley

30 minutes prior to end of cooking time, add mushrooms, and, if you opt, tomatoes. Serve in individual au gratin dishes and garnish with sprigs of parsley.

*chicken breasts may be substituted for veal fillets.

escargot in caps

spinach salad

veal birds

scalloped
mushrooms
and almonds

pinot noir

APPETEASER
walnut stuffed mushrooms

PIECE DE NO RESISTANCE
variations in veal

ON THE SIDE
scalloped mushrooms
and almonds

gamay beaujolais

DESSERT
varies daily,
ask your server

VARIATIONS IN VEAL

Your experimental nature is sure to be noticed with this unusual entree. May your seductive effort reap a variety of rewards.

STEP ONE: 25 min.

2 T. butter
1 1/2 lb. boned veal shoulder, cubed
1/4 C. brandy

1/2 C. raisins
1/4 C. brandy

Melt butter in large fry pan and brown veal. Heat brandy in small pan and ignite, pour over veal. When flame dies, remove veal to bowl. Meanwhile, put raisins in brandy to soak.

STEP TWO: 2 hrs.

2 T. butter
1/4 C. onion, minced
3 T. flour
1 C. strong coffee
1/2 C. chicken broth

Melt butter in same pan and saute onion for 3 min. Remove from heat and whisk in flour, coffee, and broth until blended. Remove raisins from brandy and add brandy to sauce. Return to heat and boil, stirring until thickened. Add veal and raisins. Cover and simmer 1 1/2 hrs.

STEP THREE: 3 min.

1/2 C. sour cream
1 t. tarragon
sprigs of parsley
2 C. cooked noodles

Remove veal to au gratin dishes, in which you have a bed of noodles. Stir in sour cream and tarragon. Heat thoroughly but do not boil. Spoon sauce over all and garnish with parsley sprigs.

GETTING HOT CHOPS

But don't show it, your partner may get cold feet!

STEP ONE: 1 hr. 25 min.

4-6 loin chops, trimmed **2 T. flour** **salt and pepper** **2 T. butter** **1/4 C. white wine** **1 T. lemon juice**	Dry chops with paper towels. Shake flour, salt, and pepper in a plastic bag. Add chops and shake to coat. Melt butter in large fry pan and brown chops over medium heat 8-10 min. per side. Add wine and juice. Cover and simmer on low heat 1 hr.

STEP TWO: 10 min.

1 1/2 T. flour **1 C. cream** **2 T. Dijon mustard** **a dash of cayenne** **sprigs of parsley**	Remove chops to au gratin dishes and keep warm. Whisk flour into pan drippings (after removing any lumps of fat), add cream, mustard, and cayenne. Bring mixture to a boil, stirring constantly. Pour sauce over chops and garnish with parsley.

hot and sweet

suggestive salad

brandied sweet potatoes

getting hot chops

sauvignon blanc

fresh garden salad

ginger glazed carrots

wild rice with almonds

the folly of eve

riesling

THE FOLLY OF EVE

Adam didn't mind at all when she put it to him this way . . .

STEP ONE: 20 min.

4-6 pork chops
1 T. shortening

Brown chops in shortening over medium heat for 8-10 minutes per side.

STEP TWO: 2 hrs. 20 min.

2 apples, cored and sliced
1/2 t. cinnamon
1/4 C. brown sugar
2 T. butter
3/4 C. sherry

Arrange pork chops in a greased casserole. Layer apples over chops and sprinkle with cinnamon and brown sugar. Dot with butter and pour sherry over all. Cover and bake at 325° for 1 1/2 hrs.

STEP THREE: 3 min.

sprigs of parsley

Arrange chops in two au gratin dishes, place apple slices over them and spoon sauce over all. Garnish with parsley sprigs.

PASSIONS A LA PECHE

The Romans called him Cupid, the Greeks called him Eros.Whatever you call him, passion was his game. This sweet melding of flavors will nurture your lover's passion to incomparable excess.

STEP ONE: 1 hr. 20 min.

4-6 pork chops
salt and pepper, to taste
1 C.green onions, sliced
1 can cream of chicken soup
1/4 C. white wine
1 1/2 t. prepared mustard
1 can sliced peaches (drain and reserve syrup)

Season chops with salt and pepper. Brown in a lightly greased pan over medium heat 8-10 min. per side. Add onion and continue cooking until tender. Stir in soup, wine, broth, mustard, and syrup. Bring to a boil, cover and simmer 45 min.

STEP TWO: 50 min.

peaches
sprigs of parsley

Add peaches and heat through. Place chops into au gratins and arrange peaches on top. Pour sauce over all and garnish with parsley.

chilled salad

fresh asparagus

brandied sweet potatoes

passions a la pêche

chenin blanc

APPETEASER
escargot in caps

LETTUCE BE LOVERS
artichoke crown salad

ON THE SIDE
glazed acorn squash

PIECE DE NO RESISTANCE
lusty lapin

fume blanc

DESSERT
only if you can
keep the pace

LUSTY LAPIN

*Rabbits have a habit
and you will, too,
we all know what rabbits do . . .*

STEP ONE: 20 min.

3 T. butter
1 cut-up rabbit

Melt butter in large fry pan and brown rabbit slowly over medium heat.

STEP TWO: 20 min.

1 clove garlic, chopped
2 medium onions, sliced
1 T. flour, rounded
1 C. white wine
2 C. chicken broth
6 cherry tomatoes

Remove rabbit from pan. Add garlic and onion, saute 5 min. Add flour, with whisk, and cook over low heat until browned. Add wine and broth. Bring to boil. Add tomatoes.

STEP THREE: 2 hr.

1/2 t. thyme
2 bay leaves
2 T. parsley, chopped
1/2 t. salt
1/2 t. pepper
1/2 C. mushroom caps
sprigs of parsley

Season sauce and return rabbit to pan. Liquid should just cover rabbit, if not, add broth. Simmer 1 1/2 to 2 hr. Add mushrooms during last 20 min. of cooking time. Arrange rabbit in individual au gratin dishes, pour sauce over rabbit and garnish with parsley sprigs.

NAUGHTY OR NICE NAVARIN MOUTON

Either or both, it's for you to decide.

STEP ONE: 2 hrs.

1-1 1/2 lb. lamb, cubed
2 small onions, quartered
2 large carrots, sliced
1 can new potatoes
1 bay leaf
1 T. lemon juice
3 C. water
1 C. mushrooms, sliced
salt and pepper, to taste

Place all ingredients, except mushrooms, into a dutch oven. Bring to a boil, cover, and simmer 1 1/2-2 hrs. Add mushrooms 20 min. prior to the end of cooking time. Remove lamb and vegetables to covered serving dish, and keep warm.

STEP TWO: 20 min.

3 T. butter
6 T flour

Reduce cooking liquid to 2 1/2 cups, by boiling it. In saucepan, melt butter and add flour while stirring constantly. Add the cooking liquid slowly, while stirring and simmer 5 minutes.

STEP THREE: 10 min.

1 egg yolk
1/2 C. cream

Blend yolk and cream. Add a little sauce and blend. Stir this mixture into the saucepan and heat thoroughly. Pour sauce over meat and vegetables. Serve.

APPETEASER
escargot in caps

LETTUCE BE LOVERS
marinated vegetables

PIECE DE NO RESISTANCE
naughty or nice
navarin mouton

sauvignon blanc

DESSERT
house specialty
served nice or naughty

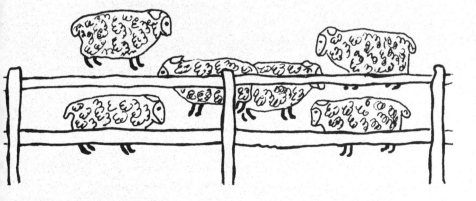

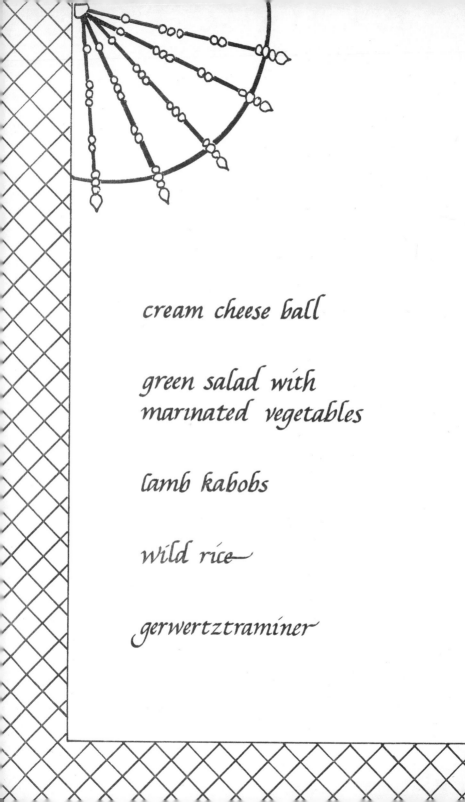

cream cheese ball

green salad with
marinated vegetables

lamb kabobs

wild rice

gerwertztraminer

MARINATED LAMB KABOBS . . .

(or Barbs, or Bills, or Betties)

STEP ONE: 30 min.

1 pkg. **frozen brussel sprouts, cooked**
2 C. **fresh whole mushrooms**
2 C. **cherry tomatoes**
8 **small white boiling onions, peeled**
1 to 1 1/2 lb. **boneless lamb shoulder, cubed**
1 lb. **bacon, raw**

Place all ingredients into large bowl or a rectangular dish.

STEP TWO: 60 min.

1 C. **oil**
1/4 C. **lemon juice**
2 **cloves garlic, crushed**
1/4 t. **thyme**

Mix all ingredients together and pour over vegetables and meats. Marinate 1 hr. or more.

STEP THREE: 60 min.

Starting with bacon, thread meat and vegetables on skewers, interlacing bacon over and under each piece. Broil 5" from heat for 30 min. turn and baste for even browning.

SOMETHING ON THE SIDE

SCALLOPED MUSHROOMS AND ALMONDS

STEP ONE: 4 min.

1/2 C. slivered almonds

Place almonds in a small fry pan over lowest heat and toast, stirring constantly.

STEP TWO: 10 min.

1 C. mushrooms, sliced
1/2 C. butter
1 C. half and half

Saute mushrooms in butter until tender, approximately 5 minutes. Add half and half and bring to a simmer.

STEP THREE: 8 min.

2 T. flour
salt and pepper, to taste
2 T. parsley, chopped
2 sprigs of parsley

Shake flour and water in a jar until well-blended. Add to pan, stirring constantly, until thickened. Add almonds, salt, and pepper. Sprinkle parsley over all and spoon into small au gratins. Garnish with sprigs of parsley. (This may be kept warm in the oven. When ready to serve, add milk to sauce if needed.)

BRANDIED SWEET POTATOES

STEP ONE: 5 min.

1/2 C. walnuts, chopped
1/4 C. butter

Saute walnuts in butter until lightly toasted. Remove walnuts from pan.

STEP TWO: 5 min.

1/2 C. brown sugar
1/2 t. salt
1/2 C. orange juice*
1/2 t. grated orange peel

Add remaining ingredients to pan and bring to a boil for 3-4 min. Reduce heat and return walnuts to pan.

STEP THREE: 10 min.

1 can sweet potatoes, cut to bite-size

Add sweet potatoes to sauce and stir to coat. Heat thoroughly and transfer to serving bowl or small au gratins.

STEP FOUR: 2 min.

1/4 C. brandy

Heat brandy in small pan, until bubbles form around edge of brandy. Pour brandy over sweet potatoes and ignite. Serve flaming.

*juice from canned peaches or apricots may be substituted for orange juice.

BROCCOLI IN LEMON SAUCE

STEP ONE: 15 min.

1/2 bunch fresh broccoli, cut up

Micro-cook or steam broccoli until tender.

STEP TWO: 5 min.

2 T. butter
1 T. flour
1/2 C. milk

Melt butter in small fry pan and gradually whisk in flour. Slowly add milk, stirring constantly, to avoid lumps.

STEP THREE: 2 min.

1 t. grated lemon peel
1 T. lemon juice
1/4 t. ginger
1/4 t. salt

Gradually add lemon peel and lemon juice, then add ginger and salt. Stir until well-blended.

STEP FOUR: 2 min.

lemon slices (make one slice from center of lemon to edge of peel then twist the lemon).

Transfer broccoli to small au gratins or serving dish and spoon sauce over it. Garnish with lemon slices.

HONEY GLAZED ACORN SQUASH

STEP ONE: 20 min.

1 medium acorn squash	Cut squash in half and remove seeds. Steam or micro-cook until tender.

STEP TWO: 20 min.

1/4 C. butter, melted	Combine all ingredients, blending well.
1/4 t. ginger	Turn squash right-side up in baking dish
1/4 t. cinnamon	and fill cavities with sauce. Be sure to
1/4 t. salt	spoon some sauce over tops and sides of
1/4 C. honey	squash. Bake at 350° for 15 min. Baste
1/4 C. walnuts, chopped	once.

GINGER GLAZED CARROTS

STEP ONE: 5 min.

3-4 medium carrots, sliced	Steam or micro-cook carrots until tender.

STEP TWO: 4 min.

1/4 C. butter	In small saucepan, melt butter, stir in
1/4 C. honey	honey and ginger. Add carrots and stir
1/2 t. ginger	to coat. Toss with parsley and serve.
1 T. parsley, minced	

INDEX

NAUGHTY NOTES

NAUGHTY NOTES